Editor
Eric Migliaccio

Managing Editor
Ina Massler Levin, M.A.

Editor-in-Chief
Sharon Coan, M.S. Ed.

Cover Artist
Janet Chadwick

Art Manager
Kevin Barnes

Art Director
CJae Froshay

Imaging
Rosa C. See

Product Manager
Phil Garcia

Publisher
Mary D. Smith, M.S. Ed.

Author

Debra J. Housel, M.S. Ed.

Teacher Created Resources, Inc.
6421 Industry Way
Westminster, CA 92683
www.teachercreated.com
ISBN: 978-0-7439-3775-7

©2003 Teacher Created Resources, Inc.
Reprinted, 2008
Made in U.S.A.

The classroom teacher may reproduce copies of materials in this book for classroom use only. The reproduction of any part for an entire school or school system is strictly prohibited. No part of this publication may be transmitted, stored, or recorded in any form without written permission from the publisher.

Table of Contents

Introduction 3

Spelling Lessons

    Lesson 1—Comparisons of Two.. 4

    Lesson 2—Comparisons with More than Two 6

    Lesson 3—Word Beginning: "in" 8

    Lesson 4—Word Beginning: "ex" 10

    Lesson 5—Word Beginning: "re" 12

    Lesson 6—Word Beginning: "pre" 14

    Lesson 7—Word Beginning: "con" 16

    Lesson 8—Word Parts: "ist" & "ic" 18

    Lesson 9—Word Ending: "ish" 20

    Lesson 10—Word Endings: "ard" & "ier" 22

    Lesson 11—Word Ending: "tive" 24

    Lesson 12—Word Ending: "ant" 26

    Lesson 13—Word ending: "ance" 28

    Lesson 14—Word Ending: "ture" 30

    Lesson 15—Word Ending: "ity" 32

    Lesson 16—Word Ending: "lar" 34

    Lesson 17—Word Ending: "ful" 36

    Lesson 18—Word Ending: "ent" 38

    Lesson 19—Word Ending: "ence" 40

    Lesson 20—Word Endings: "ia," "ian," & "ious" 42

Assessments 44

Answer Key 46

Introduction

The old adage "practice makes perfect" can really hold true for your child's education. The more practice and exposure your child has with concepts being taught in school, the more success he or she is likely to find. As a parent, it is difficult to know where to focus your efforts so that the extra practice your child receives at home supports what he or she is learning in school.

This book has been written to help parents and teachers reinforce basic skills with children. *Practice Makes Perfect: Spelling* covers basic spelling skills for fifth graders. The exercises in this book can be completed in any order. The practice lessons will meet or reinforce educational standards and objectives similar to the ones required by your state and school district for fifth graders:

- The student will know the spelling patterns for comparison words.
- The student will recognize the spelling patterns for common word beginnings and endings.
- The student will accurately spell words with multiple syllables.
- The student will spell high-frequency words, the 3,000 words that make up more than 90 percent of all written material. High-frequency words make up the majority of the spelling words in each lesson.

Since educational research has shown that memorizing syllables is the best way to learn to spell words with multiple syllables, each lesson shows the syllabication of the words based on *The American Heritage Dictionary*.

How to Make the Most of This Book

Here are some ideas for making the most of this book:

- Set aside a specific place in your home to work on this book. Keep it neat and tidy, with the necessary materials on hand.
- Determine a specific time of day to work on these practice pages to establish consistency. Look for times in your day or week that are less hectic and more conducive to practicing skills.
- Keep all practice sessions with your child positive and constructive. If he or she becomes frustrated or tense, do not force your child to perform. Set the book aside and try again another time.
- Review and praise the work your child has done.
- Allow the child to use whatever writing instrument he or she prefers. For example, writing with gel pens on black paper adds variety and pleasure to drill work.
- Introduce the spelling words in the list. Discuss how the words are different and how they are alike. Read the "In Context" column together. Be sure that the student understands the meaning of each word.
- Have the child memorize each word in chunks. Study the syllables shown in each lesson and practice putting the pieces together.
- If necessary, help the student to read and comprehend the directions and exercises.
- Encourage the child to point out spelling words, past and present, in the books, newspapers, and magazines he or she reads.

Lesson 1: Comparisons of Two

Comparisons of Two

Adjectives describe nouns. They give details. Adjectives help you to form a picture in your mind. **Example:** The *dark*, *swirling* cloud quickly moved nearer to the *old* barn.

Rules:
- Adjectives that compare two things usually have the letters "e" and "r" near the end.
- If the adjective already ends in "e," just add an "r." **Example:** large ➡ larger
- If the adjective has a short vowel followed by a single consonant, first double the consonant, then add the ending. **Example:** hot ➡ hotter
- If the adjective ends in "y" and compares two or more things, drop the "y" and add "ier." **Example:** messy ➡ messier

Word	Syllables	In Context
better	bet•ter	I think your idea is **better** than mine.
more	more	Would you like some **more** coffee?
worse	worse	Instead of going away, the fever got **worse**.
farther	far•ther	Sam lives **farther** away from me than Jill does.
closer	clo•ser	Move the end table **closer** to the couch.
rougher	rough•er	This piece of sandpaper is **rougher** than that piece.
bigger	big•ger	My brother is **bigger** than most of the other kids his age.
faster	fast•er	I won the race because I ran **faster** than the others.
slower	slow•er	Going by train is **slower** than going by plane.
younger	young•er	Her **younger** sister just learned how to read.
shorter	short•er	Bill is **shorter** than Jack.
easier	ea•si•er	She thinks it's **easier** to read another language than to speak it.
dirtier	dir•ti•er	Now the car looked **dirtier** than when we started to wash it!
uglier	ug•li•er	That dress is much **uglier** than the one you already have.
scarier	scar•i•er	The second movie is even **scarier** than the first.

Write the spelling word that is an **antonym** (opposite) of the word given.

Example: quieter   noisier

1. farther   shorter
2. less   more
3. better   worse
4. smoother   rougher
5. prettier   uglier
6. older   younger
7. funnier   sader
8. smaller   bigger
9. cleaner   dirtier
10. worse   better
11. closer   farther
12. faster   slower
13. harder   softer
14. taller   shorter
15. slower   faster

Lesson 1: Comparisons of Two

Comparisons of Two *(cont.)*

Different Kinds of Sentences

Write spelling words 1–5 in **exclamatory** sentences. An exclamatory sentence communicates strong emotion or surprise. **Example:** *We've got to get out of the store right away!*

Exclamatory Sentences End with an Exclamation Point

1. _____
2. _____
3. _____
4. _____
5. _____

Write spelling words 6–10 in **declarative** sentences. A declarative sentence makes a statement. **Example:** *We went to the store.*

Declarative Sentences End with a Period

6. _____
7. _____
8. _____
9. _____
10. _____

Write spelling words 11–15 in **interrogative** sentences. An interrogative sentence asks a question. **Example:** *Did you go to the store?*

Interrogative Sentences End with a Question Mark

11. _____
12. _____
13. _____
14. _____
15. _____

© Teacher Created Resources, Inc.   #3775 Practice Makes Perfect: Spelling—Grade 5

Lesson 2: Comparisons with More than Two

Comparisons with More than Two

Adjectives describe nouns and give details. **Example:** The *scary* dragon showed its *sharp* teeth.
Rules:

- Adjectives that compare three or more things have the letters "e," "s," and "t" near the end.
- If the adjective already ends in "e," just add "st." **Example:** *close* ➡ *closest*
- If the adjective has a short vowel followed by a single consonant double the consonant, then add the ending. **Example:** *hottest*
- If the adjective ends in "y" and compares three or more things, drop the "y" and add "iest." **Example:** *scary* ➡ *scariest*

Word	Syllables	In Context
most	most	The present she wants the **most** is a puppy.
best	best	Her **best** friend moved away last week.
worst	worst	This storm was the **worst** to hit the state in 50 years.
farthest	far•thest	The **farthest** I can walk in one day is 20 miles.
largest	lar•gest	The blue box was the **largest** one in the pile.
loudest	loud•est	Those fireworks were the **loudest** I've ever heard.
saddest	sad•dest	That's the **saddest** face I've ever seen. What's wrong?
longest	long•est	The **longest** river in the U.S. is the Mississippi River.
biggest	big•gest	Jenny's cat is the **biggest** one on our street.
tallest	tall•est	Ian is the **tallest** kid in our class.
happiest	hap•pi•est	Her wedding day was the **happiest** day of her life.
friendliest	friend•li•est	I picked this hamster because it was the **friendliest** one.
noisiest	nois•i•est	In the **noisiest** room, we saw preschool children playing.
tiniest	ti•ni•est	My bedroom is the **tiniest** one in our house.
driest	dri•est	A desert has the **driest** environment in the world.

Underline the word that's spelled correctly. Copy it on the line.

1. tinyest   tinest   tiniest   _____
2. longest   longgest   longist   _____
3. bigest   biggest   biggist   _____
4. noisyest   noisiest   noisest   _____
5. worst   worsest   wurst   _____
6. sadest   saddist   saddest   _____
7. driest   dryest   drist   _____
8. loudiest   loudest   loudist   _____
9. friendlest freindliest friendliest _____
10. largst   largest   largeest   _____
11. tallest   talest   tallist   _____
12. moest   most   mostest   _____
13. fartherest farthist   farthest   _____
14. beist   best   bestest   _____
15. happiest   happist   happyest   _____

Lesson 2: Comparisons with More than Two

Comparisons with More than Two (cont.)

Identifying Synonyms and Antonyms

Copy the spelling words in order in the first column. Look at the word in the second column. Decide if each pair of words are **synonyms** (similar in meaning) or **antonyms** (opposite in meaning). Put a check mark (✓) in one of the last two columns to indicate your choice. You may use a thesaurus or dictionary to look up the meaning of the spelling word.

Spelling Word	Word	Synonym	Antonym
Example: ugliest	prettiest		✓
1.	least		
2.	worst		
3.	best		
4.	closest		
5.	biggest		
6.	noisiest		
7.	happiest		
8.	shortest		
9.	largest		
10.	shortest		
11.	unhappiest		
12.	unfriendliest		
13.	quietist		
14.	smallest		
15.	wettest		

Lesson 3: "in"

Word Beginning: "in"

Word	Syllables	In Context
increase	in•crease	Running seems to **increase** my appetite.
indicate	in•di•cate	Please **indicate** which time you prefer on the enclosed card.
invited	in•vi•ted	Jamie **invited** the whole class to her party.
industry	in•dus•try	In Detroit making auto parts is the major **industry**.
involved	in•volved	Do you plan to get **involved** in the school play?
individual	in•di•vid•u•al	Every **individual** needs his or her own kit.
industrial	in•dus•tri•al	The **industrial** part of town has factories.
introduced	in•tro•duced	Dawn **introduced** him to her parents.
interior	in•te•ri•or	The box's **interior** was lined with blue satin.
intended	in•tend•ed	I **intended** to clean the house before you arrived.
innocent	in•no•cent	You are presumed **innocent** until proven guilty.
invented	in•ven•ted	Thomas Edison **invented** the electric light bulb.
ingredient	in•gre•di•ent	My dad's recipes always have some secret **ingredient**.
inadequate	in•ad•e•quate	His light jacket was **inadequate** against the bitter wind.
independent	in•de•pen•dent	As the baby learned to walk, he became more **independent**.

Copy the spelling words in the order they appear above. Number them in order from A–Z. You may need to look as far as the third letter. Then write the words in A–Z order.

	Word	Number	A–Z Order
1.			
2.			
3.			
4.			
5.			
6.			
7.			
8.			
9.			
10.			
11.			
12.			
13.			
14.			
15.			

Lesson 3: "in"

Word Beginning: "in" (cont.)

Crossword Puzzle

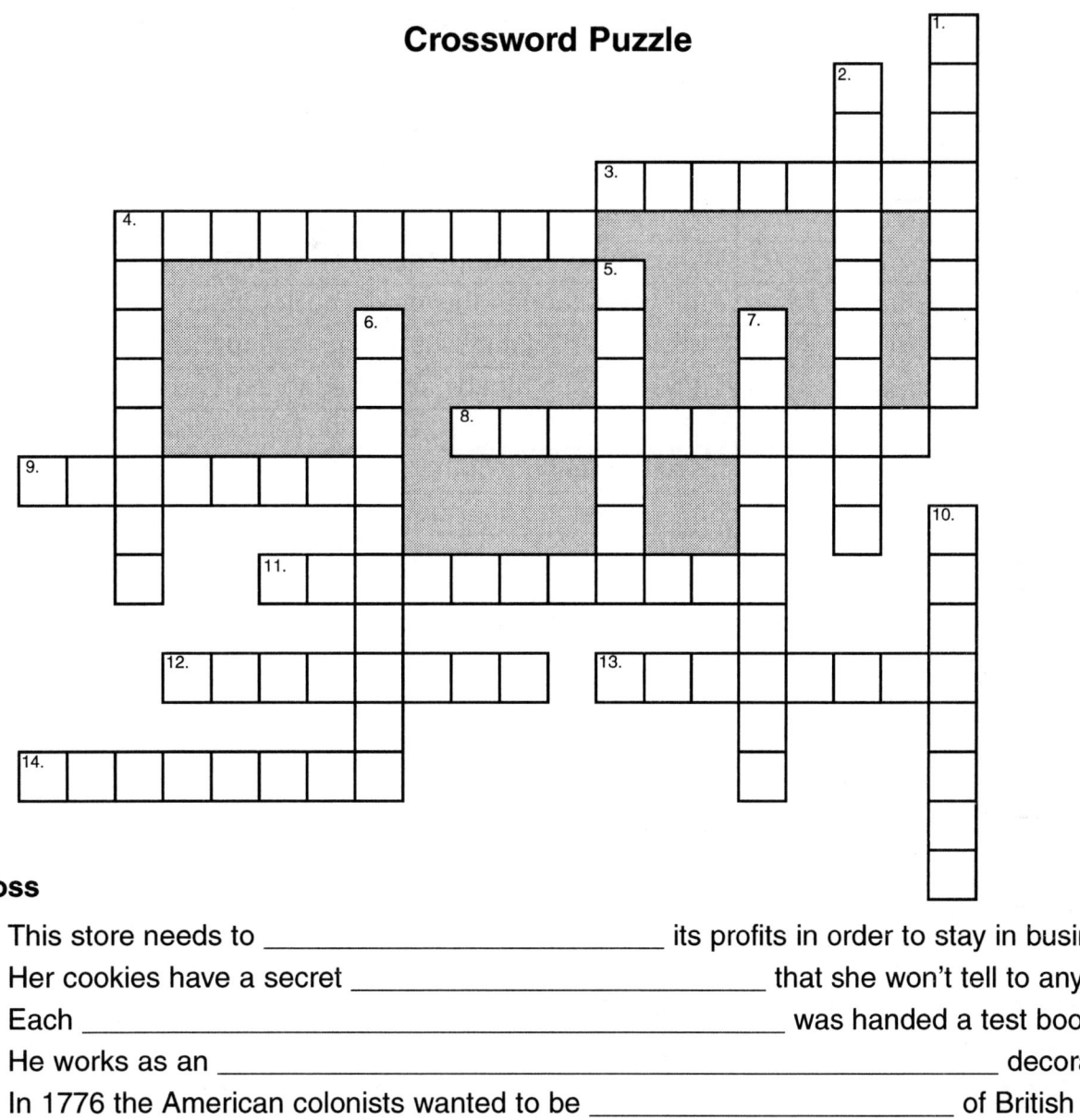

Across

3. This store needs to _____ its profits in order to stay in business.
4. Her cookies have a secret _____ that she won't tell to anyone.
8. Each _____ was handed a test booklet.
9. He works as an _____ decorator.
11. In 1776 the American colonists wanted to be _____ of British rule.
12. The jury found the woman _____ of the murder charges.
13. Please _____ the size that you'd like to order.
14. Were you _____ in Saturday night's robbery?

Down

1. Alexander Graham Bell _____ the telephone.
2. Fifteen minutes will be an _____ amount of time to finish this job.
4. The computer _____ is constantly changing and growing.
5. Jeri _____ all of the girls to her slumber party.
6. Brett _____ his sister to Mrs. Sojo.
7. Since this area is zoned _____, no houses will be built here.
10. I had not _____ to speak so sharply.

© Teacher Created Resources, Inc. 9 #3775 Practice Makes Perfect: Spelling—Grade 5

Lesson 4: "ex"

Word Beginning: "ex"

Word	Syllables	In Context
exercise	ex•er•cise	Daily **exercise** will help you to have a healthy body.
except	ex•cept	I'd go with you, **except** I'm already going somewhere else.
exciting	ex•ci•ting	This is the most **exciting** carnival I've ever seen!
excuse	ex•cuse	You'll need a doctor's **excuse** to sit out of gym class.
expected	ex•pect•ed	My mom **expected** me home an hour ago.
examine	ex•am•ine	After you **examine** this gem, you'll want to have it.
explorer	ex•plor•er	Christopher Columbus is a famous **explorer**.
expand	ex•pand	They're having a baby and need to **expand** their home.
exclaimed	ex•claimed	"What in the world are you doing?" Lisa **exclaimed**.
extremely	ex•treme•ly	It's **extremely** hot in the desert.
exchange	ex•change	She needs to **exchange** the shirt for a larger size.
expert	ex•pert	He's an **expert** on fossils.
excellent	ex•cel•lent	You did an **excellent** job with your class presentation.
exception	ex•cep•tion	It seems like there's an **exception** to every spelling rule.
excitement	ex•cite•ment	The children couldn't hide their **excitement**.

Is the **boldfaced** word spelled wrong? If it is not correct, write it correctly in the middle column. If it is correct, circle **OK**.

1. Let me **examin** that coin more closely.		OK
2. Loren is an **expert** deep sea diver.		OK
3. Marco Polo is a famous **explorer**.		OK
4. The food at their restaurant is **excellent**.		OK
5. Cory **exclaimed**, "Wait! I want to come, too!"		OK
6. What **exscuse** did he give for not showing up?		OK
7. I had **expected** you to come later.		OK
8. Is there ever an **exeption** to the rule?		OK
9. The farmer bought more land to **expand** his orchards.		OK
10. They had an **exciting** day at the race track.		OK
11. It was **extremely** cold here last February.		OK
12. There was a sense of **excitment** in the air.		OK
13. We get to **exersise** during gym class.		OK
14. Please **exchange** papers with a classmate.		OK
15. Your report is perfect **exsept** for this sentence.		OK

Lesson 4: "ex"

Word Beginning: "ex" (cont.)

Word Scramble

Unscramble the words below to form spelling words from this lesson. Put the numbered letters on the lines below to find the answer to the riddle.

Example: etrax   e   x   t   r   a

1. pedeetxc   __ __ __ __ __ __ __ __
2. dapenx   __ __ __ __₁ __ __
3. texper   __ __ __ __₂ __ __
4. cintgixe   __ __ __ __ __ __ __ __
5. clextenle   __ __ __ __ __ __ __ __ __
6. treelymex   __ __ __ __ __ __ __ __₃ __
7. cesexu   __ __ __ __₄ __ __
8. criesexe   __ __ __ __ __ __ __₅ __
9. declaimxe   __ __ __ __ __ __ __₆ __ __
10. ecpxet   __ __ __ __ __ __₇
11. xepetcoin   __ __ __ __ __ __ __₈ __ __
12. nxagceeh   __ __ __ __₉ __ __ __ __
13. lporexre   __ __ __ __ __ __₁₀ __ __
14. maxinee   __ __ __ __ __ __₁₁ __
15. meettcixen   __ __₁₂ __ __ __ __ __ __ __ __

Riddle: What increases its value by half when it's flipped upside down?

__ __ __   __ __ __ __ __ __ __   __ __ __
7   9   2   11   4   6   2   10   1   3   5   8   12

© Teacher Created Resources, Inc.   #3775 Practice Makes Perfect: Spelling—Grade 5

Lesson 5: "re"

Word Beginning: "re"

The word beginning "re" is most often pronounced with a **long /e/**.

Word	Syllables	In Context
reduced	re•duced	Robert **reduced** the size of the peg to fit it in the hole.
remember	re•mem•ber	What do you **remember** from our trip to Florida?
recent	re•cent	It has rained a lot in **recent** weeks.
result	re•sult	As a **result** of the rain, a house was flooded.
required	re•qui•red	The remote-control car **required** four batteries.
regards	re•gards	This message **regards** the purchase I made last week.
repair	re•pair	The rusty old flute was in need of **repair**.
remarkable	re•mark•a•ble	Zoe got **remarkable** grades on her report card.
resources	re•sour•ces	This area is rich in coal and other natural **resources**.
research	re•search	The scientist's **research** led to a cure.
relief	re•lief	The doctor gave Jonah pain **relief** medicine.
refrigerator	re•frig•er•a•tor	Paul took some cheese from the **refrigerator**.

Sometimes a word beginning with "re" means "again," as in *redo* (to do again).

Word	Syllables	In Context
recall	re•call	The company may **recall** the car.
rename	re•name	You need to **rename** that file.
rewrite	re•write	John had to **rewrite** his entire report.

Choose the best word from the list above to complete each sentence. Write it on the line. Use each word once. Skip those you can't figure out and go back to them once you've done the others.

1. Sunlight and wind are both renewable energy _____.
2. This project is the end _____ of all of her hard work.
3. I'm going to _____ the dog I got from the shelter.
4. Our _____ isn't keeping food cold anymore; we need a new one.
5. Help me to _____ to set my alarm clock to 6 A.M.
6. The test is over. What a _____!
7. In the past few years, cancer _____ has made great progress.
8. Zach made a _____ recovery.
9. To get a library card in my county, proof of your address is _____.
10. Give my _____ to your parents.
11. Act now! Our prices have been _____ up to 40 percent!
12. If you want full credit, you must _____ the assignment by tomorrow.
13. Kyle enjoyed your _____ visit to his home.
14. Unfortunately, their car needs a major _____.
15. Do you _____ where you were on September 18th?

Lesson 5: "re"

Word Beginning: "re" (cont.)

Dictionary Word Sort

Parts of Speech

- **Nouns:** people, places, or things—such as *restaurant*, *recruit* (person), and *record* (physical file)
- **Verb:** action words—such as *realize*, *reject*, *recommend*, *recruit*, and *record* (to make a record)
- **Adjectives:** words that describe and give details—such as *real* and *reasonable*

Use a dictionary to sort this lesson's spelling words by their parts of speech. The parts of speech will appear in italics and be abbreviated *v*, *n*, and *adj*. Write each spelling word inside the correct circle. *Words that can be used as more than one part of speech must be written inside the appropriate circles' intersection.*

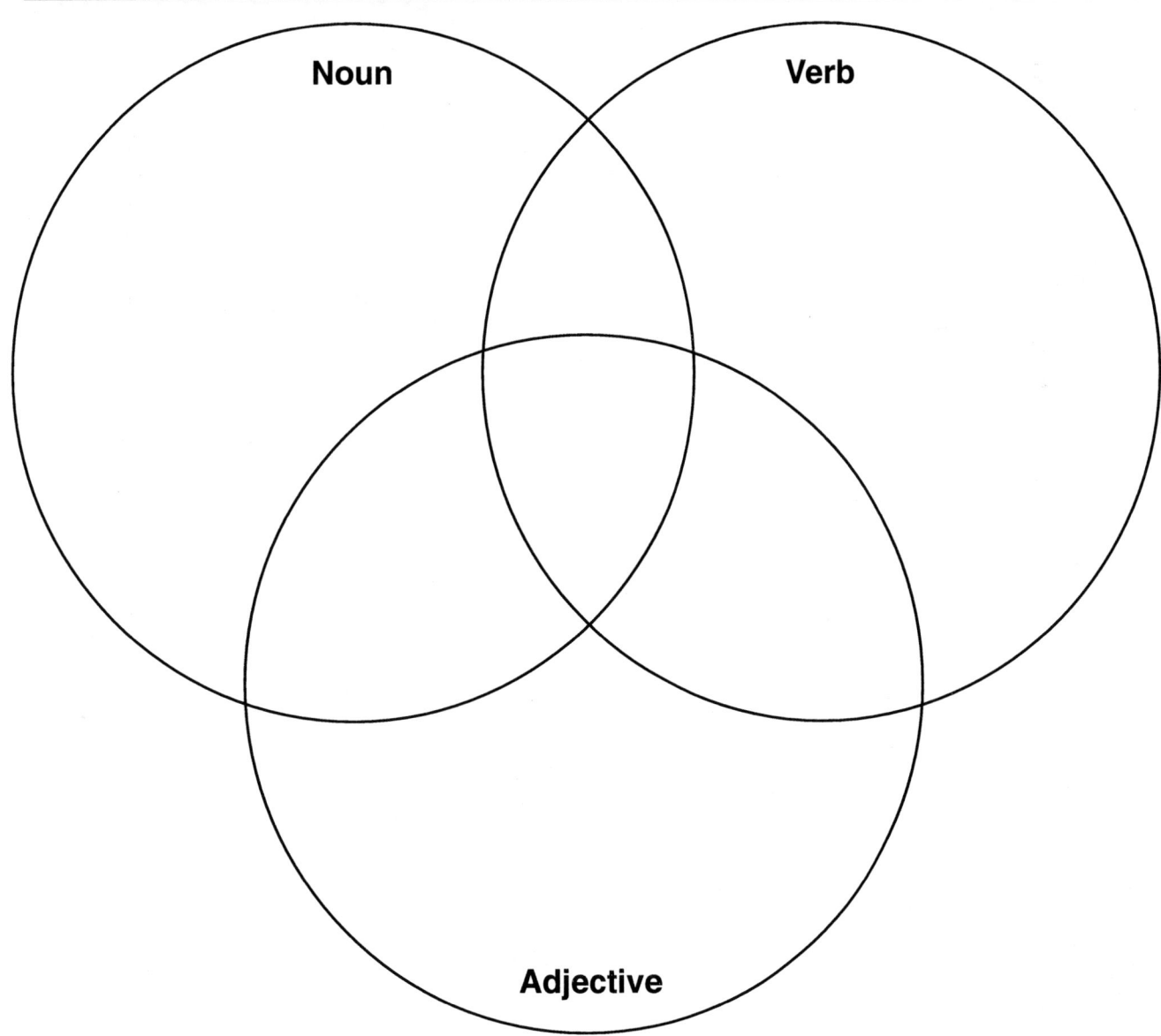

Lesson 6: "pre"

Word Beginning: "pre"

The word beginning "pre" may be pronounced with a **long** or **short /e/**, depending on the word. Try pronouncing each of the spelling words. Do you know what each one means?

Word	Syllable	In Context
prepared	pre•pared	The woman **prepared** the meal.
prevent	pre•vent	Washing your hands helps to **prevent** the spread of germs.
preferred	pre•ferred	You told me that you **preferred** to leave on Wednesday.
preceding	pre•ced•ing	The band was **preceding** the floats in the parade.
precise	pre•cise	Nobody knows the **precise** time a volcano will erupt.
presence	pres•ence	Your **presence** at the funeral will comfort the family.
presents	pres•ents	Did you get a lot of **presents** on your birthday?
preoccupied	pre•oc•cu•pied	He was so **preoccupied** with school that he couldn't think.
pretend	pre•tend	Let's **pretend** we're knights in a castle.
prejudice	prej•u•dice	Judging before you know all of the facts is **prejudice**.

When the "pre" is pronounced with a **long /e/**, it often means "before."

Word	Syllable	In Context
predict	pre•dict	I **predict** that it will snow tomorrow.
prepaid	pre•paid	Send it in this **prepaid** envelope.
preschool	pre•school	He went to **preschool** when he was three years old.
precaution	pre•cau•tion	Turn off the electricity as a **precaution**.
premature	pre•ma•ture	The **premature** baby was born three weeks early.

Write the spelling word that fits the clue given. Each word is used once.

Clue	Matches With Spelling Word?
Example: a short connecting word	preposition
1. when others judge you before they even know you	
2. you may have gone here when you were 3 or 4	
3. you've given these at birthday parties	
4. you liked one better than the other	
5. you hope to do this with crimes and accidents	
6. your contest entry coming before another entry	
7. you bought tickets in advance of the show	
8. just your being there is important	
9. you're not acting the way you really feel	
10. you had everything necessary to do the job	
11. you couldn't stop thinking about something	
12. your measurements need to be exact	
13. why your home has a smoke detector	
14. you tried to do something way too soon	
15. you guess the number before rolling the dice	

Lesson 6: "pre"

Word Beginning: "pre" *(cont.)*

Syllable Cymbals

Write each spelling word on the cymbal that matches its number of syllables. Write the syllables within each word using different colors.

Lesson 7: "con"

Word Beginning: "con"

Word	Syllables	In Context
controlling	con•trol•ling	The owner was having trouble **controlling** his dog.
consider	con•sid•er	Smokers should **consider** the dangers of smoking.
conditions	con•di•tions	Foggy **conditions** made it hard to see.
connected	con•nec•ted	The hotel is **connected** to the mall.
contact	con•tact	You can **contact** me at home.
concerned	con•cerned	I'm **concerned** about your health.
convinced	con•vinced	She's not **convinced** that the cat needs an operation.
concert	con•cert	My brother's **concert** is tonight.
container	con•tain•er	The nails are stored in that red **container**.
continue	con•tin•ue	Before you **continue**, fill out this form.
conflict	con•flict	The **conflict** caused the neighbors to stop speaking.
contribute	con•trib•ute	They will **contribute** their time and money to a good cause.
conserve	con•serve	We must **conserve** the world's natural resources.
construction	con•struc•tion	Hard hats are worn at the **construction** site.
conversation	con•ver•sa•tion	He hoped to overhear their **conversation**.

Is the **boldfaced** word spelled wrong? If it is not correct, write it correctly in the middle column. If it is right, circle **OK**.

1. Can you **contribute** $2 to the fund?		OK
2. Should these parts be **conected**?		OK
3. The weather **conditions** made travel difficult.		OK
4. I'm very **conserned** about her poor grades.		OK
5. The remote is **controling** the television.		OK
6. We want to **continue** doing business with you.		OK
7. There is often **conflick** in the Middle East.		OK
8. He's not **convinced** that the toy is beyond repair.		OK
9. Do you have time for a long phone **convesation**?		OK
10. Our spring **consert** is on April 5.		OK
11. Cody will **contact** his senator.		OK
12. Let's try harder to **conserve** fuel.		OK
13. In which **containner** is it stored?		OK
14. Did you **consider** the other ideas, too?		OK
15. That **construction** site is dangerous!		OK

Lesson 7: "con"

Word Beginning: "con (cont.)

Crack the Code!

Find the code to form the spelling words in this lesson.

Example: <u>Y</u> <u>R</u> <u>K</u> <u>P</u> <u>B</u> <u>U</u> <u>S</u> <u>W</u> <u>Q</u> <u>X</u> <u>R</u> <u>K</u>
          c o n s e r v a t i o n

In this code, "Y" always stands for "c." The example gives the code for 10 letters. Fill in those letters below. Next, decode the longest words first. As you figure out a new letter, write it everywhere it appears on the page.

1. Y R K Y B U K B A _____ concerned

2. Y R K Q U R H H X K D _____ controlling

3. Y R K S X K Y B A _____ convinced

4. Y R K P X A B U _____ consider

5. Y R K A X Q X R K P _____ conditions

6. Y R K Y B U Q _____ concert

7. Y R K K B Y Q B A _____ connected

8. Y R K Q W X K B U _____ container

9. Y R K Q W Y Q _____ contact

10. Y R K Q X K Z B _____ continue

11. Y R K S B U P W Q X R K _____ conversation

12. Y R K P B U S B _____ conserve

13. Y R K C H X Q _____ conflict

14. Y R K P Q U Z Y Q X R K _____ construction

15. Y R K Q U X F Z Q B _____ contribute

Lesson 8: "ist" & "ic"

Spelling Patterns: "ist" & "ic"

Both of these common spelling patterns have the **short /i/** sound.

Word	Syllables	In Context
exists	ex•ists	If such a place **exists**, I'd have heard about it.
distant	dis•tant	He saw a light shining on a **distant** shore.
insisted	in•sis•ted	She **insisted** on leaving the hospital after only two days.
assistant	as•sis•tant	The doctor's **assistant** gave the baby some medicine.
scientist	sci•en•tist	The **scientist** made an important discovery.
picnic	pic•nic	Let's take a **picnic** to the park.
traffic	traf•fic	The **traffic** jam made us three hours late.
specific	spe•cif•ic	I don't know what you mean. Can you be more **specific**?
mechanic	me•chan•ic	Our car was fixed by an auto **mechanic**.
electronic	e•lec•tron•ic	An **electronic** device beeped when it needed a new battery.
automatic	au•to•mat•ic	He got money from the **automatic** teller machine.
historic	his•tor•ic	The **historic** building was turned into a museum.
realistic	re•al•is•tic	It's not **realistic** to expect to lose ten pounds a week.
optimistic	op•ti•mis•tic	An **optimistic** person looks for the good in any situation.
characteristics	char•ac•ter•is•tics	Animals are grouped based on their **characteristics**.

Underline the word that's spelled correctly. Copy it on the line.

1. optomistic   optumistic   optimistic   _____
2. mechanic   mekanic   machinc   _____
3. charteristics   characteristics   charatestics   _____
4. reallistic   realisstic   realistic   _____
5. assistant   asistant   assistent   _____
6. hisstoric   hisotric   historic   _____
7. ellectronic   electronic   elctronic   _____
8. picknic   piknic   picnic   _____
9. traffic   trafic   traffick   _____
10. exists   exissts   exsists   _____
11. distent   distant   distunt   _____
12. specfic   spesific   specific   _____
13. autamatic   autumatic   automatic   _____
14. insisted   insited   inzisted   _____
15. sientist   sceintist   scientist   _____

Lesson 8: "ist" & "ic"

Spelling Patterns: "ist" & "ic" *(cont.)*

Crossword Puzzle

Across

2. I need _____ directions in order to find my way there.
6. When women received the right to vote, it was an _____ moment.
8. She asked her _____ to make the copies.
9. I could see the smoke rising from the chimney of a _____ cabin.
11. It's such a beautiful day that we should go on a _____ .
14. Genes determine the traits, or _____ , that your parents pass on to you.
15. She wants to study chemistry in order to become a _____ .

Down

1. It's not _____ to try to stay awake for 72 hours straight.
3. The boy _____ that he didn't know anything about the robbery.
4. A computer is an _____ device.
5. The _____ was backed up for two miles.
7. Let's try to be _____ about her chances for recovery.
10. My car's _____ transmission has stopped working.
12. The car _____ had to jack up the car in order to repair it.
13. If the Loch Ness monster really _____ , why hasn't anyone gotten a clear photograph?

Lesson 9: "ish"

Word Ending: "ish"

Word	Syllables	In Context
English	En•glish	The **English** language has many unusual spellings.
Spanish	Span•ish	**Spanish** is the most common language spoken in South America.
furnish	fur•nish	I'd like to **furnish** my room with painted furniture.
publish	pub•lish	Our school plans to **publish** a newspaper.
polish	pol•ish	Please **polish** the furniture.
foolish	fool•ish	She felt **foolish** because she didn't know the right answer.
selfish	self•ish	By refusing to share with his friends, he's acting **selfish**.
vanish	van•ish	I can't find my jacket. It just seemed to **vanish**.
punish	pun•ish	He had to **punish** the child for biting.
relish	rel•ish	I like to put **relish** on my hamburger.
establish	es•tab•lish	Let's **establish** some rules before we begin.
diminish	di•min•ish	Once the rain starts to **diminish**, I'll go.
distinguish	dis•tin•guish	From this distance, can you **distinguish** between the two girls?
accomplish	ac•com•plish	He will **accomplish** a lot if he keeps working at it.
astonished	as•ton•ished	When the door burst open, the woman was **astonished**.

Choose the best word from the list above to complete each sentence. Write it on the line. Use each word once. Skip those you can't figure out and go back to them once you've done the others.

1. It would be _____ to stick your hand into an alligator's mouth.
2. News reports are usually given in _____ in the U.S.A.
3. These colors are so similar that it's hard to _____ between them.
4. He decided to _____ a club for people who own hedgehogs.
5. They will _____ their newsletter on the first of each month.
6. We plan to _____ our family room with wicker furniture.
7. I was _____ when I heard about the accident.
8. The principal will _____ the naughty child.
9. Ramon acted _____ when he refused to share his candy.
10. Do you like sweet or dill _____ on your hamburger?
11. Your keys have to be here. They couldn't just _____!
12. Did you _____ all that you had hoped you would?
13. Many people in Puerto Rico read, write, and speak both English and _____.
14. Belinda will _____ the silver until it shines.

Lesson 9: "ish"

Word Ending: "ish" *(cont.)*

Different Kinds of Sentences

Write spelling words 1–5 in **exclamatory** sentences. An exclamatory sentence communicates strong emotion or surprise. **Example:** *We've got to get out of the store right away!*

Exclamatory Sentences End with an Exclamation Point

1. _____
2. _____
3. _____
4. _____
5. _____

Write spelling words 6–10 in **declarative** sentences. A declarative sentence makes a statement. **Example:** *We went to the store.*

Declarative Sentences End with a Period

6. _____
7. _____
8. _____
9. _____
10. _____

Write spelling words 11–15 in **interrogative** sentences. An interrogative sentence asks a question. **Example:** *Did you go to the store?*

Interrogative Sentences End with a Question Mark

11. _____
12. _____
13. _____
14. _____
15. _____

Lesson 10: "ard" & "ier"

Word Endings: "ard" & "ier"

- The word ending "ard" is usually pronounced "erd."
- The word ending "ier" is pronounced "E-yur."

Word	Syllables	Context
forward	for•ward	The truck slowly moved **forward**.
standard	stan•dard	The **standard** treatment for a cold is lots of fluids and rest.
afterwards	af•ter•wards	They drank hot chocolate **afterwards**.
cupboard	cup•board	Please put the dishes in the **cupboard**.
toward*	to•ward	Jack looked **toward** the raging bull.
awkward	awk•ward	Sitting in such low seats felt **awkward**.
hazard	haz•ard	Plugging too many cords into one outlet is a fire **hazard**.
orchard	or•chard	The workers picked the peaches in the **orchard**.
pier	pier	The **pier** was destroyed by the ocean's pounding waves.
glacier	gla•cier	A **glacier** is a slow-moving thick sheet of ice.
frontier	fron•tier	On the **frontier**, "neighbors" were often miles apart.
cashier	cash•ier	A **cashier** rang up the sale.
soldier	sol•dier	The **soldier** raised the flag.
barrier	bar•ri•er	Road workers put up a **barrier** to stop traffic.
photocopier	pho•to•cop•i•er	Use the **photocopier** to make ten copies.

* Ending is pronounced "ord." *Towards* is also correct, but *toward* is the preferred usage.

Write the spelling word that begins and ends with same letters as the word given. Each spelling word is used just once. Since the spelling words *pier* and *photocopier* begin and end with the same letters, use each one just once. The first one has been done for you.

1. pepper   _____pier_____
2. horrid   _____
3. atlas   _____
4. toad   _____
5. sheer   _____
6. odd   _____
7. ashamed   _____
8. sand   _____
9. barter   _____
10. card   _____
11. glamour   _____
12. cracker   _____
13. food   _____
14. farther   _____
15. professor   _____

Lesson 10: "ard" & "ier"

Word Endings: "ard" & "ier" *(cont.)*

Identifying Synonyms and Antonyms

Copy the spelling words in order in the first column. Look at the word in the second column. Decide if each pair of words are **synonyms** (similar in meaning) or **antonyms** (opposite in meaning). Put a check mark (✓) in one of the last two columns to indicate your choice. You may use a thesaurus or dictionary to look up the meaning of the spelling word.

Spelling Word	Word	Synonym	Antonym
Example: messier	neater		✓
1.	backward		
2.	unusual		
3.	before		
4.	cabinet		
5.	away		
6.	comfortable		
7.	danger		
8.	grove		
9.	dock		
10.	lava		
11.	city		
12.	sales clerk		
13.	civilian		
14.	blockade		
15.	printer		

© Teacher Created Resources, Inc.

Lesson 11: "tive"

Word Ending: "tive"

Despite the "e" at the end, the word ending "tive" is pronounced with a **short /i/**.

Word	Syllables	In Context
native	na•tive	These plants are **native** to Asia.
active	ac•tive	At 86 she still leads a very **active** life.
negative	neg•a•tive	Don't have a **negative** attitude.
positive	pos•i•tive	It's good to say something **positive** about other people.
effective	ef•fec•tive	The medicine was **effective**, and she recovered quickly.
relatives	rel•a•tives	She went to pick up her **relatives** at the airport.
motive	mo•tive	The police don't know the **motive** for the crime.
adjective	ad•jec•tive	An **adjective** adds details about a noun.
sensitive	sen•si•tive	Don't be harsh; her feelings are **sensitive**.
attractive	at•trac•tive	That furniture is very **attractive**.
detective	de•tec•tive	The **detective** secretly followed the man.
executive	ex•ec•u•tive	The **executive** went to the meeting.
talkative	talk•a•tive	He is so **talkative** that I'm tired of listening to him.
competitive	com•pet•i•tive	They offer a **competitive** salary.
representatives	rep•re•sen•ta•tives	We elect **representatives** to govern our country.

Is the **boldfaced** word spelled wrong? If it is not correct, write it correctly in the middle column. If it is right, circle **OK**.

1. What was his **motive**?		OK
2. Are you **postive** you turned the lights off?		OK
3. The **detective** collected evidence at the scene.		OK
4. The toddler was very **active**.		OK
5. A word describing size, shape, or color is an **ajective**.		OK
6. My **relatives** are coming to visit this Christmas.		OK
7. Does she think that artwork is **atractive**?		OK
8. Keep **negtive** comments to yourself.		OK
9. Team sports are **competitive**.		OK
10. Our company president's office is the **excutive** suite.		OK
11. Is this anti-itch cream **effective**?		OK
12. Most people are **senstive** to criticism.		OK
13. Each state elects two senators as **representatives**.		OK
14. He's not very **talkative**.		OK
15. I'm a **nattive** of Kenya.		OK

Lesson 11: "tive"

Word Ending: "tive" *(cont.)*

Word Scramble

Unscramble the words below to form spelling words from this lesson. Put the numbered letters on the lines below to find the answer to the riddle.

Example: epacevithyr <u>h</u> <u>y</u> <u>p</u> <u>e</u> <u>r</u> <u>a</u> <u>c</u> <u>t</u> <u>i</u> <u>v</u> <u>e</u>
                          1   2

1. tomvie   ___ ___ ___ ___ ___ ___
                                 3

2. tivesrepsenreta   ___ ___ ___ ___ ___ ___ ___ ___ ___ ___ ___ ___ ___ ___
                                                       4

3. cuteexive   ___ ___ ___ ___ ___ ___ ___ ___ ___
                                   5

4. laerstiev   ___ ___ ___ ___ ___ ___ ___ ___ ___
                         6

5. ipetcomtive   ___ ___ ___ ___ ___ ___ ___ ___ ___ ___ ___

6. gavetine   ___ ___ ___ ___ ___ ___ ___ ___
                        7

7. tracatveit   ___ ___ ___ ___ ___ ___ ___ ___ ___ ___
                                 8

8. eectvdiet   ___ ___ ___ ___ ___ ___ ___ ___ ___
                                 9

9. vectfefei   ___ ___ ___ ___ ___ ___ ___ ___ ___
                                     10

10. steinsiev   ___ ___ ___ ___ ___ ___ ___ ___ ___
                       11

11. jadtecive   ___ ___ ___ ___ ___ ___ ___ ___ ___
                              12

12. ivecat   ___ ___ ___ ___ ___ ___

13. ivattlake   ___ ___ ___ ___ ___ ___ ___ ___ ___
                     13

14. ispitvoe   ___ ___ ___ ___ ___ ___ ___ ___
          14

15. tanive   ___ ___ ___ ___ ___ ___
       15

Riddle: What animals are the most generous?

___ ___ ___ ___ ___ ___ .   ___ ___ ___ ___ ___ ___ ___ ___ ___ ___ ___ ,   ___ ___ ___ ___
11 13 5 15 13 11   12 1 3 2 6 6   7 9 10 3

___ ___ ___ ___ ___ ___   ___ (___) ___ ___ ___ ___
 4 15 2 14 15 3   4   11   8 3 15 12

Lesson 12: "ant"

Word Ending: "ant"

The word ending "ant" is usually pronounced "Uhnt" in multi-syllable words.

Word	Syllables	In Context
important	im•por•tant	What's so **important** that you had to get me up at 3 A.M.?
instant	in•stant	This camera takes **instant** photos that develop immediately.
infant	in•fant	The **infant** was quite tiny.
pleasant	pleas•ant	She has a **pleasant** personality.
constant	cons•tant	The flow of cars past our house was **constant**.
servant	ser•vant	He became a **servant** in the mansion.
brilliant	bril•liant	She often has **brilliant** ideas.
relevant	rel•e•vant	I don't see how that question is **relevant**.
hydrant	hy•drant	Never block a fire **hydrant**.
elegant	el•e•gant	She looked **elegant** in the silver gown.
fragrant	fra•grant	The flowers were very **fragrant**.
immigrant	im•mi•grant	He's an **immigrant** from China.
restaurant	res•tau•rant	What **restaurant** would you like to go to?
significant	sig•nif•i•cant	Does the mistake seem very **significant**?
extravagant	ex•trav•a•gant	They spent an **extravagant** amount of money.

Choose the best word from the list above to complete each sentence. Write it on the line. Use each word once. Skip those you can't figure out and go back to them once you've done the others.

1. She spent the _____ sum of $100,000 for her wedding gown.
2. It's _____ to us that you feel completely comfortable.
3. Please leave out any details that aren't _____.
4. The crystal dishes made the table look especially _____.
5. The firefighters were upset to find the _____ frozen shut.
6. The Afghan _____ needs to learn a new language.
7. She hired him as her household _____.
8. Your perfume is particularly _____.
9. The error was not _____, since it was hardly noticeable.
10. The bulb's light was _____.
11. Their _____ daughter is just nine days old.
12. The _____ loud noise made the cat nervous.
13. Where's your favorite Chinese _____ located?
14. Chatting online is a form of _____ communication.
15. We had a _____ conversation about our pets.

Lesson 12: "ant"

Word Ending: "ant" (cont.)

Identifying Synonyms and Antonyms

Copy the spelling words in order in the first column. Look at the word in the second column. Decide if each pair of words are **synonyms** (similar in meaning) or **antonyms** (opposite in meaning). Put a check mark (✓) in one of the last two columns to indicate your choice. You may use a thesaurus or dictionary to look up the meaning of the spelling word.

Spelling Word	Word	Synonym	Antonym
Example: merchant	seller	✓	
1.	unimportant		
2.	slow		
3.	adult		
4.	nasty		
5.	frequent		
6.	maid		
7.	stupid		
8.	irrelevant		
9.	water main		
10.	fancy		
11.	foul		
12.	traveler		
13.	café		
14.	insignificant		
15.	sufficient		

Lesson 13: "ance"

Word Ending: "ance"

When a short word ends with "ance," it usually sounds like "ants."

Word	Syllables	In Context
glance	glance	She left without a backward **glance**.
chance	chance	Here's our **chance** to score some goals.
advance	ad•vance	Each year you **advance** to the next grade level.

When a multi-syllable word ends with "ance," it sounds like "UHnce."

Word	Syllables	In Context
distance	dis•tance	We could hear sirens in the **distance**.
instance	ins•tance	In this **instance**, I wouldn't say anything.
balance	bal•ance	They struggled to **balance** the budget.
ambulance	am•bu•lance	An **ambulance** raced to the scene.
appearance	ap•pear•ance	She gave the **appearance** of someone wealthy.
importance	im•por•tance	I can't stress enough the **importance** of knowing how to write.
performance	per•for•mance	He gave an amazing **performance**.
resistance	re•sis•tance	The soldiers met with **resistance** from the villagers.
entrance	en•trance	There's the **entrance** to the building.
tolerance	tol•er•ance	It's important to show **tolerance** of others' beliefs.
appliance	ap•pli•ance	She traded in her old **appliance** for a new one.
guidance	guid•ance	The **guidance** counselor suggested the change.

Copy the spelling words in the order they appear above. Number them in order from A–Z. You may need to look as far as the third letter. Then write the words in A–Z order.

	Word	Number	A–Z Order
1.			
2.			
3.			
4.			
5.			
6.			
7.			
8.			
9.			
10.			
11.			
12.			
13.			
14.			
15.			

Lesson 13: "ance"

Word Ending: "ance" (cont.)

Using a Dictionary

Guide words are in bold print at the top of each dictionary page. You look at them to see if the word you want falls *between* them.

Write each spelling word. Look up each one in a dictionary. What are the two guide words at the top of the page? Write the guide words.

Spelling Word	Left-Side Guide Word	Right-Side Guide Word
Example: dance	dalmatian	dare
1.		
2.		
3.		
4.		
5.		
6.		
7.		
8.		
9.		
10.		
11.		
12.		
13.		
14.		
15.		

Lesson 14: "ture"

Word Ending: "ture"

The word ending "ture" is not pronounced the way it looks: it is pronounced "chur."

Word	Syllables	In Context
nature	na•ture	In **nature** all wild animals are part of a food web.
future	fu•ture	No one knows what will happen in the **future**.
mixture	mix•ture	Stir the **mixture** well before adding the chocolate chips.
captured	cap•tured	The boy finally **captured** his missing lizard.
features	fea•tures	The book **features** many beautiful color photos.
creatures	crea•tures	As the only flying mammals, bats are unusual **creatures**.
structure	struc•ture	The **structure** looked as if a light wind could knock it down.
temperature	tem•per•a•ture	Most people don't like the **temperature** to go above 95°F.
miniature	min•i•a•ture	He made a **miniature** village to go with his train set.
agriculture	ag•ri•cul•ture	Farmers work in the field of **agriculture**.
literature	lit•er•a•ture	*Alice in Wonderland* is a famous piece of children's **literature**.
signature	sig•na•ture	The form required a parent's **signature**.
furniture	fur•ni•ture	They went to buy some **furniture** for their new house.
adventure	ad•ven•ture	Going on vacation is always an **adventure**.
moisture	mois•ture	The **moisture** caused mold to grow.

Write the spelling word that fits the clue given. Each word is used once.

Clue	Matches With Spelling Word?
Example: place to insert a light bulb	fixture
1. in the air on a foggy day	
2. caught; trapped	
3. tiny	
4. can be hot, cold, or just right	
5. a check can't be cashed without this	
6. being out in the woods, away from civilization	
7. tomorrow, in a week, next month	
8. tables, chairs, couches, beds	
9. a great book by an important author	
10. doing something new and exciting; escapade	
11. a house, a barn, or a skyscraper	
12. living beings	
13. cookie dough before it's cooked	
14. traits; qualities, characteristics	
15. dairy farms, crops, farm animals	

Lesson 14: "ture"

Word Ending: "ture" (cont.)

Syllable Cymbals

Write each spelling word on the cymbal that matches its number of syllables. Write the syllables within each word using different colors.

Lesson 15: "ity"

Word Ending: "ity"

The word ending "ity" is pronounced "ih-tee."

Word	Syllables	In Context
community	com•mu•ni•ty	The whole **community** decorated the town.
electricity	e•lec•tric•i•ty	Ben Franklin proved that lightning was **electricity**.
quality	qual•i•ty	All of our **quality** clothing is made of the best fabrics.
quantity	quan•ti•ty	A large **quantity** of snow had fallen overnight.
university	u•ni•ver•si•ty	My brother attends an out-of-state **university**.
ability	a•bil•i•ty	She has natural singing **ability**.
gravity	grav•i•ty	Everything falls to the ground because of **gravity**.
opportunity	op•por•tu•ni•ty	Would you like an **opportunity** to work this weekend?
majority	ma•jor•i•ty	The **majority** of people voted for him.
curiosity	cu•ri•os•i•ty	He read her diary out of **curiosity**.
personality	per•son•al•i•ty	People tell me that he has a friendly **personality**.
authority	au•thor•i•ty	A school principal is an **authority** figure.
capacity	ca•pac•i•ty	The room's **capacity** is 120 people.
similarity	sim•i•lar•i•ty	The two paintings' **similarity** is amazing.
responsibility	res•pon•si•bil•i•ty	As citizens, we have a **responsibility** to vote.

Circle the word that's spelled correctly. Copy it on the line.

1. quontity / quantity / quanity _____
2. authority / autherity / athority _____
3. oportunity / opportunity / oppotunity _____
4. capcity / cappacity / capacity _____
5. comunity / community / communnity _____
6. responsibility / responsbility / responsiblity _____
7. ability / ablity / abality _____
8. gravety / gravitty / gravity _____
9. unversity / university / univirsity _____
10. elictricity / electricity / eletricity _____
11. majority / magority / mejority _____
12. similarty / simlarity / similarity _____
13. curiousity / curiosity / cureosity _____
14. personalty / personelity / personality _____
15. quality / quaility / quailty _____

Lesson 15: "ity"

Word Ending: "ity" (cont.)

Word Scramble

Unscramble the words below to form spelling words from this lesson. Put the numbered letters on the lines below to find the answer to the riddle.

Example: polarutiyp   p o p u l a r i t y

1. yvgaitr   _ _ _ _ _ _
        1
2. laqutiy   _ _ _ _ _ _
           2
3. yporttonuip   _ _ _ _ _ _ _ _ _ _
           3
4. sitvineyur   _ _ _ _ _ _ _ _ _
              4
5. ityiocurs   _ _ _ _ _ _ _ _
           5
6. pityacac   _ _ _ _ _ _ _ _
                    6
7. antyquit   _ _ _ _ _ _ _ _
                       7
8. htraityou   _ _ _ _ _ _ _ _
            8
9. itysonpearl   _ _ _ _ _ _ _ _ _ _
              9
10. mintumcoy   _ _ _ _ _ _ _ _ _
                       10
11. itrailmyis   _ _ _ _ _ _ _ _ _ _
               11
12. lisponresybiti   _ _ _ _ _ _ _ _ _ _ _ _ _ _
                 12
13. cityeectri   _ _ _ _ _ _ _ _ _ _
            13
14. baitlyi   _ _ _ _ _ _ _
         14
15. jamitory   _ _ _ _ _ _ _ _
    15

Riddle: What did one math book say to the other?

_ _ _ , _ _ _ _ _ _ _ _ _
14 9 7   8 2 4 13   10   1 9 6

_ _ _ _ _ _ _ _ !
3 5 9 14 11 13 15 12

Lesson 16: "lar"

Word Ending: "lar"

The letters "lar" usually come at the end of a word and sound as if they're spelled "ler."

Word	Syllables	In Context
molar	mo•lar	A **molar** is one of the large teeth in the back of the mouth.
solar	so•lar	The word **solar** means "sun."
polar	po•lar	The **polar** bear chased the seal.
burglar	bur•glar	A **burglar** broke into my home and took my computer.
dollars	dol•lars	It will cost nine **dollars** to fix it.
collar	col•lar	The man grabbed the boy's **collar**.
cellar	cel•lar	I don't like to go down into the **cellar** after dark.
cellular	cel•lu•lar	She used her **cellular** phone to make the call.
regular	reg•u•lar	The **regular** price is $69.99; the sale price is $49.99.
irregular	ir•reg•u•lar	The jeans cost less because they had an **irregular** seam.
similar	sim•i•lar	Your shirt is **similar** to mine.
popular	pop•u•lar	She's nice to everyone, which is why she's so **popular**.
particular	par•tic•u•lar	Is there any **particular** size you're looking for?
spectacular	spec•tac•u•lar	We saw a **spectacular** view from the top of the mountain.
caterpillar	cat•er•pil•lar	A **caterpillar** will turn into a moth or a butterfly.

Choose the best word from the list above to complete each sentence. Write it on the line. Use each word once. Skip those you can't figure out and go back to them once you've done the others.

1. The _____ wanted to be sure that nobody was home.
2. People confuse us because we looks so _____.
3. A total _____ eclipse doesn't happen as often as a lunar eclipse.
4. He's a _____ boy because he's so friendly.
5. My lower _____ hurt so badly that my jaw ached.
6. The fuzzy _____ was brown and black.
7. Do you want a _____ color, or will any color do?
8. If the _____ ice caps were to melt, the world's ocean levels would rise.
9. How many _____ have you saved?
10. She went to see the doctor about her _____ heartbeat.
11. The old house's _____ had a dirt floor.
12. That show was so good that I'd call it _____.
13. The bus's _____ arrival time is 11:00.
14. Can you repair this shirt's _____?
15. The people did not want the _____ phone tower built near their homes.

Lesson 16: "lar"

Word Ending: "lar" (cont.)

Using a Dictionary

> Guide words are in bold print at the top of each dictionary page. You look at them to see if the word you want falls *between* them.

Write each spelling word. Look up each one in a dictionary. What are the two guide words at the top of the page? Write the guide words.

Spelling Word	Left-Side Guide Word	Right-Side Guide Word
Example: muscular	multicultural	music
1.		
2.		
3.		
4.		
5.		
6.		
7.		
8.		
9.		
10.		
11.		
12.		
13.		
14.		
15.		

Lesson 17: "ful"

Word Ending: "ful"

The word ending "ful" means "full of." However, it is spelled with just one "l."

Word	Syllables	In Context
awful	aw•ful	We came as soon as we heard the **awful** news.
beautiful	beau•ti•ful	The waterfall was very **beautiful**.
useful	use•ful	The gate was not **useful** because the dog could jump over it.
wonderful	won•der•ful	That song that you wrote is **wonderful**!
powerful	pow•er•ful	A **powerful** bolt of lightning struck the tree.
successful	suc•cess•ful	She was **successful** in finding a job.
cheerful	cheer•ful	The old man was always **cheerful** and smiling.
peaceful	peace•ful	After the noise of the city, the forest seemed very **peaceful**.
doubtful	doubt•ful	He felt **doubtful** that he would get to school on time.
painful	pain•ful	The flu shot was not **painful**.
harmful	harm•ful	Smoking is **harmful**.
thankful	thank•ful	The **thankful** Pilgrims held a feast.
hopeful	hope•ful	I feel **hopeful** that studying will help me to pass the test.
plentiful	plen•ti•ful	The orange crop was **plentiful** last year.
graceful	grace•ful	Those ballet dancers are **graceful**.

Write the spelling word that is an **antonym** (opposite) of the word given. You may use a dictionary or thesaurus, if necessary.

Example: careless _____careful_____

1. hopeless _____
2. unsuccessful _____
3. certain _____
4. weak _____
5. ungrateful _____
6. ugly _____
7. sad _____
8. painless _____

9. scarce _____
10. useless _____
11. clumsy _____
12. terrible _____
13. beneficial _____
14. violent _____
15. terrific _____

Lesson 17: "ful"

Word Ending: "ful" *(cont.)*

Understanding Word Meaning

Copy the spelling words in order in the first column. Write what each one means in the second column, following the example below. Then write the word again.

Word	Means	Word
Example: careful	full of care	careful
1.		
2.		
3.		
4.		
5.		
6.		
7.		
8.		
9.		
10.		
11.		
12.		
13.		
14.		
15.		

16. How does adding the ending "ful" to the base words plenty and beauty differ from adding "ful" to the other base words in this list? _____

_____

© Teacher Created Resources, Inc.   #3775 Practice Makes Perfect: Spelling—Grade 5

Lesson 18: "ent"

Word Ending: "ent"

Word	Syllables	In Context
different	dif•fer•ent	Is there a **different** way to solve the problem?
present	pres•ent	Have you chosen a **present** for Kim yet?
represent	rep•re•sent	Joe will **represent** our class at the spelling match.
events	e•vents	What **events** are on your calendar for this month?
recent	re•cent	The robotic lawn mower is a **recent** invention.
silent	si•lent	When the class fell **silent**, the teacher began to speak.
accident	ac•ci•dent	Fortunately, nobody was hurt in the **accident**.
patient	pa•tient	You need to be **patient** when training a dog.
president	pres•i•dent	The club **president** ran each meeting.
students	stu•dents	How many **students** are in your class?
evident	ev•i•dent	It soon became **evident** that they were in love.
current	cur•rent	News reports give **current** events.
ancient	an•cient	In **ancient** times few people knew how to read or write.
continent	con•ti•nent	One country takes up the entire **continent** of Australia.
convenient	con•ven•ient	Call me whenever it's **convenient** for you.

Is the **boldfaced** word spelled wrong? If it is not correct, write it correctly in the middle column. If it is right, circle **OK**.

1. Is Terri **present**?		OK
2. Call me when it's **conveinent** for you to do so.		OK
3. Do you know of any upcoming community **events**?		OK
4. People call the Australian **contintent** the "land down under."		OK
5. If he was angry, it was certainly not **evident**.		OK
6. There are many **diferent** colors to choose from.		OK
7. Our class often discusses **curent** events.		OK
8. These athletes **represent** the U.S.A. in the Olympics.		OK
9. George Washington was the first **president** of the U.S.A.		OK
10. The dog had an **acident** on the carpeting.		OK
11. Sandra just checked in as a **patient** in this hospital.		OK
12. The man carefully lifted the **ancient** vase.		OK
13. If we stay **sillent**, no one will know that we're hiding here.		OK
14. Mrs. Bennett's class had 26 **students**.		OK
15. I saw a **rescent** newspaper article about that subject.		OK

Lesson 18: "ent"

Word Ending: "ent" (cont.)

Different Kinds of Sentences

Write spelling words 1–5 in exclamatory sentences. An exclamatory sentence communicates strong emotion or surprise. **Example:** *We've got to get out of the store right away!*

Exclamatory Sentences End with an Exclamation Point

1. _____
2. _____
3. _____
4. _____
5. _____

Write spelling words 6–10 in declarative sentences. A declarative sentence makes a statement. **Example:** *We went to the store.*

Declarative Sentences End with a Period

6. _____
7. _____
8. _____
9. _____
10. _____

Write spelling words 11–15 in interrogative sentences. An interrogative sentence asks a question. **Example:** *Did you go to the store?*

Interrogative Sentences End with a Question Mark

11. _____
12. _____
13. _____
14. _____
15. _____

Lesson 19: "ence"

Word Ending: "ence"

Word	Syllables	In Context
sentence	sen•tence	You need to change this into a complete **sentence**.
difference	dif•fer•ence	Can you tell the **difference** between frogs and toads?
influence	in•flu•ence	The mayor used her **influence** to get a traffic light put in.
audience	au•di•ence	The **audience** roared with laughter.
reference	ref•er•ence	We had to go to the library to use the **reference** books.
evidence	ev•i•dence	The police need more **evidence** in order to find the thief.
absence	ab•sence	You need a note to explain your **absence** yesterday.
experience	ex•pe•ri•ence	That was a frightening **experience**!
conference	con•fer•ence	My dad is going to have a **conference** with my teacher.
occurrence	oc•cur•rence	If there's another **occurrence** like this, you'll be suspended.
science	sci•ence	In **science** class, we're studying the human body.
patience	pa•tience	The father had **patience** with his whining child.
preference	pref•er•ence	We have red or blue. Do you have a **preference** in color?
intelligence	in•tel•li•gence	Information gathered about enemies is called **intelligence**.
convenience	con•ven•ience	Let's stop at the **convenience** store to get some milk.

Copy the spelling words in the order they appear above. Number them in order from A–Z. You may need to look as far as the third letter. Then write the words in A–Z order.

	Word	Number	A–Z Order
1.			
2.			
3.			
4.			
5.			
6.			
7.			
8.			
9.			
10.			
11.			
12.			
13.			
14.			
15.			

Lesson 19: "ence"

Word Ending: "ence" (cont.)

Crossword Puzzle

Across

2. We learned about the solar system in our _____ class.
3. Rats have enough _____ to learn to do tricks.
5. I'm starting to lose my _____ with this rude person.
8. Please call me at your _____ .
11. What's the _____ between the two jackets?
12. Do you have a _____ as to where you want to sit in theater?
13. The _____ started clapping as the curtain came down.
14. No one should ever drive while under the _____ of alcohol.

Down

1. No one noticed his _____ until the teacher did the class roll.
2. Please change this line; right now it's a _____ fragment.
4. A dictionary, a thesaurus, and an encyclopedia are types of _____ materials.
6. That was the third _____ of arson in six days!
7. Did you actually find any _____ that a deer had come through here?
9. Mrs. Gridstone is in an important _____ and cannot be disturbed.
10. Going to Disney World was a very exciting _____ .

Lesson 20: "ia," "ian" & "ious"

Word Endings: "ia," "ian," & "ious"

- Words ending in "ia" are pronounced "E-uh."
- Words ending in "ian" are pronounced "E-un."
- When a word ends in "ious," it is usually pronounced "E-us."

Word	Syllables	In Context
bacteria	bac•te•ri•a	Washing your hands kills many **bacteria**.
cafeteria	caf•e•te•ri•a	We took our lunch bags to the **cafeteria**.
encyclopedia	en•cy•clo•pe•di•a	Let's look up walruses in the **encyclopedia**.
librarian	li•brar•i•an	The **librarian** helped me find reference materials.
vegetarian	veg•e•tar•i•an	He's a **vegetarian** and won't eat any meat.
historian	his•to•ri•an	The town **historian** has records that are 150 years old.
various	var•i•ous	The bag was filled with **various** kinds of sweets.
curious	cu•ri•ous	The **curious** dog nudged the door open and slipped inside.
serious	se•ri•ous	The police are rushing to a **serious** accident.
obvious	ob•vi•ous	The answer is **obvious**.
furious	fu•ri•ous	The **furious** man started to shout threats.
hilarious	hi•lar•i•ous	The movie was **hilarious**, causing us to laugh a lot.
luxurious	lux•u•ri•ous	The hotel room was very **luxurious**.
mysterious	mys•te•ri•ous	The ring's **mysterious** disappearance had me baffled.
previous	pre•vi•ous	The **previous** owners painted the room red.

Write the spelling word that begins and ends with same letters as the word given. Each spelling word is used just once.

Example: gas _____glorious_____

1. lion _____
2. versus _____
3. mass _____
4. camera _____
5. hyphen _____
6. locks _____
7. orphans _____
8. paths _____

9. ballerina _____
10. hands _____
11. canvas _____
12. vein _____
13. fuss _____
14. species _____
15. era _____

Lesson 20: "ia," "ian" & "ious"

Word Endings: "ia," "ian," & "ious" (cont.)

Word Sort

Parts of Speech

- **Nouns:** people, places, or things—such as *restaurant*, *recruit* (person), and *record* (physical file)
- **Adjectives:** words that describe and give details—such as *real* and *reasonable*

Sort the spelling words in this lesson into their parts of speech. Write each spelling word inside the correct box. You may use a dictionary. The parts of speech will appear abbreviated and in italics, like this: *n.* and *adj.*

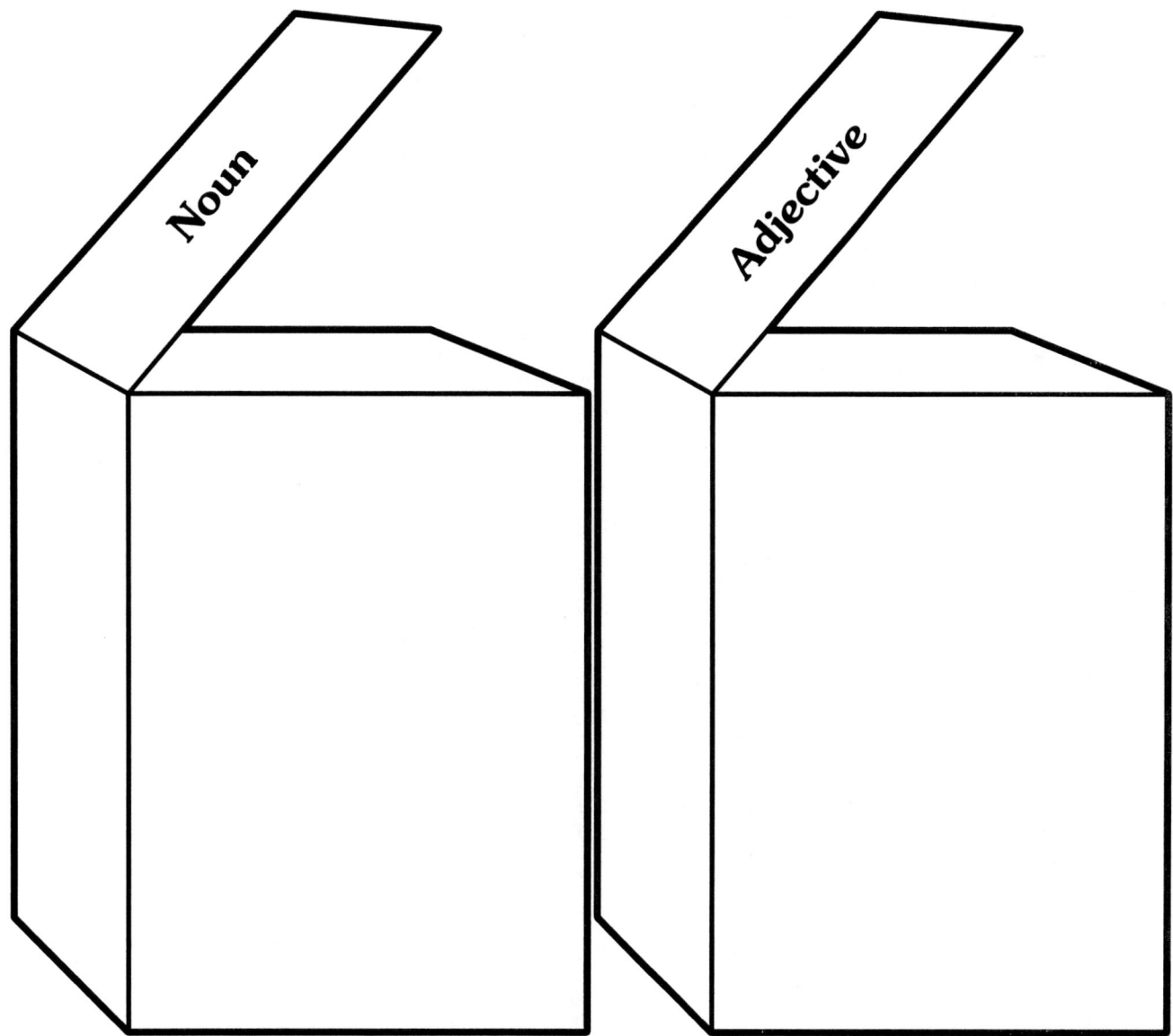

Assessment 1

Read each choice. Fill in the circle that has the underlined word spelled incorrectly. If none of the underlined choices is wrong, fill in the "e."

1.	ⓐ easier route	ⓑ connected rooms			
	ⓒ rougher surface	ⓓ postive response	ⓔ	all correct
2.	ⓐ contribute $10	ⓑ dirtier floor			
	ⓒ another ajective	ⓓ effective way	ⓔ	all correct
3.	ⓐ short conversation	ⓑ saddest face			
	ⓒ consider another	ⓓ competitive rates	ⓔ	all correct
4.	ⓐ really exsists	ⓑ pleasant smile			
	ⓒ individual letters	ⓓ noisiest child	ⓔ	all correct
5.	ⓐ distant light	ⓑ interior design			
	ⓒ best resturant	ⓓ heavy traffic	ⓔ	all correct
6.	ⓐ shared characteristics	ⓑ independant decision			
	ⓒ specific place	ⓓ her assistant	ⓔ	all correct
7.	ⓐ prefered choice	ⓑ special ingredient			
	ⓒ instant message	ⓓ historic site	ⓔ	all correct
8.	ⓐ optimistic opinion	ⓑ excellent grades			
	ⓒ strong resistence	ⓓ guest appearance	ⓔ	all correct
9.	ⓐ to furnish	ⓑ sigficant change			
	ⓒ written excuse	ⓓ establish rules	ⓔ	all correct
10.	ⓐ small creatures	ⓑ Brian exclaimed			
	ⓒ kitchen cupboard	ⓓ distingish between	ⓔ	all correct
11.	ⓐ front entrance	ⓑ guidence counselor			
	ⓒ except tomorrow	ⓓ peach orchard	ⓔ	all correct
12.	ⓐ English test	ⓑ daily exercise			
	ⓒ community fund	ⓓ various ideas	ⓔ	all correct
13.	ⓐ large glacier	ⓑ truck repair			
	ⓒ minature train	ⓓ high temperature	ⓔ	all correct
14.	ⓐ far distence	ⓑ gas appliances			
	ⓒ more capacity	ⓓ short absence	ⓔ	all correct
15.	ⓐ accomplish goals	ⓑ awkward moment			
	ⓒ negative report	ⓓ new refrigerator	ⓔ	all correct
16.	ⓐ natural resources	ⓑ another soldeir			
	ⓒ sigh of relief	ⓓ looked doubtful	ⓔ	all correct
17.	ⓐ large audience	ⓑ seemed preoccupied			
	ⓒ strong current	ⓓ hilarious story	ⓔ	all correct
18.	ⓐ coldest continent	ⓑ signature line			
	ⓒ celular phone	ⓓ nice librarian	ⓔ	all correct
19.	ⓐ child's curiousity	ⓑ western frontier			
	ⓒ remarkable recovery	ⓓ precise time	ⓔ	all correct
20.	ⓐ happiest day	ⓑ controlling the dam			
	ⓒ antique furniture	ⓓ greater conveinience	ⓔ	all correct

Assessment 2

Darken the circle of the one word that is spelled incorrectly. Read each choice before selecting.

1. ⓐ pier	ⓑ servant				
ⓒ negative	ⓓ different	ⓔ prejuidice			
2. ⓐ musclar	ⓑ forward				
ⓒ easier	ⓓ captured	ⓔ largest			
3. ⓐ ambulance	ⓑ similarity				
ⓒ creatures	ⓓ releif	ⓔ brilliant			
4. ⓐ luxurious	ⓑ required				
ⓒ accident	ⓓ quantity	ⓔ plesant			
5. ⓐ electricity	ⓑ accomplish				
ⓒ applience	ⓓ repair	ⓔ innocent			
6. ⓐ burglar	ⓑ mysterious				
ⓒ traffic	ⓓ excercise	ⓔ tolerance			
7. ⓐ responsibility	ⓑ conveinnt				
ⓒ various	ⓓ barrier	ⓔ science			
8. ⓐ awkward	ⓑ popular				
ⓒ libarian	ⓓ cafeteria	ⓔ tiniest			
9. ⓐ resourses	ⓑ bigger				
ⓒ dirtiest	ⓓ prepaid	ⓔ moisture			
10. ⓐ sensitive	ⓑ iregular				
ⓒ patient	ⓓ contribute	ⓔ ingredient			
11. ⓐ specific	ⓑ effective				
ⓒ competive	ⓓ particular	ⓔ hydrant			
12. ⓐ paitence	ⓑ awful				
ⓒ appearance	ⓓ toward	ⓔ ability			
13. ⓐ opportunity	ⓑ audience				
ⓒ historic	ⓓ exchange	ⓔ absense			
14. ⓐ happiest	ⓑ connected				
ⓒ current	ⓓ orchard	ⓔ sucessful			
15. ⓐ hopeful	ⓑ plentiful				
ⓒ encyclopedia	ⓓ remarkible	ⓔ instance			
16. ⓐ balance	ⓑ experence				
ⓒ controlling	ⓓ influence	ⓔ relevant			
17. ⓐ cellar	ⓑ Spanish				
ⓒ charateristics	ⓓ preceding	ⓔ intelligence			
18. ⓐ exception	ⓑ interior				
ⓒ optimistic	ⓓ temperture	ⓔ agriculture			
19. ⓐ spectacular	ⓑ enterance				
ⓒ convinced	ⓓ doubtful	ⓔ hilarious			
20. ⓐ occurence	ⓑ beautiful				
ⓒ signature	ⓓ consider	ⓔ resistance			

Answer Key

Page 4
1. closer
2. more
3. worse
4. rougher
5. uglier
6. younger
7. scarier
8. bigger
9. dirtier
10. better
11. farther
12. slower
13. easier
14. shorter
15. faster

Page 5
Answers will vary.

Page 6
1. tiniest
2. longest
3. biggest
4. noisiest
5. worst
6. saddest
7. driest
8. loudest
9. friendliest
10. largest
11. tallest
12. most
13. farthest
14. best
15. happiest

Page 7
1. antonym
2. antonym
3. antonym
4. antonym
5. synonym
6. synonym
7. antonym
8. antonym
9. synonym
10. antonym
11. antonym
12. antonym
13. antonym
14. synonym
15. antonym

Page 8
1. increase; 2; inadequate
2. indicate; 4; increase
3. invited; 14; independent
4. industry; 7; indicate
5. involved; 15; individual
6. individual; 5; industrial
7. industrial; 6; industry
8. introduced; 12; ingredient
9. interior; 11; innocent
10. intended; 10; intended
11. innocent; 9; interior

12. invented; 13; introduced
13. ingredient; 8; invented
14. inadequate; 1; invited
15. independent; 3; involved

Page 9

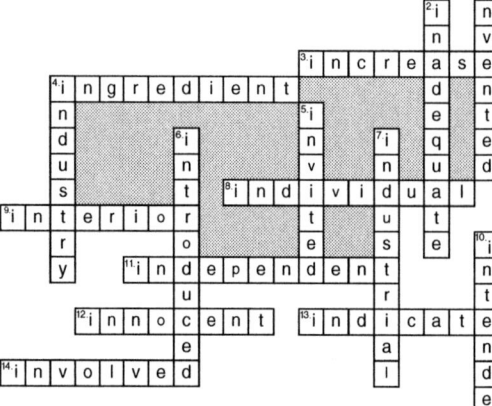

Page 10
1. examine
2. OK
3. OK
4. OK
5. OK
6. excuse
7. OK
8. exception
9. OK
10. OK
11. OK
12. excitement
13. exercise
14. OK
15. except

Page 11
1. expected
2. expand
3. expert
4. exciting
5. excellent
6. extremely
7. excuse
8. exercise
9. exclaimed
10. except
11. exception
12. exchange
13. explorer
14. examine
15. excitement

Riddle: the numeral six

Page 12
1. resources
2. result
3. rename
4. refrigerator
5. remember
6. relief
7. research
8. remarkable
9. required
10. regards
11. reduced
12. rewrite
13. recent
14. repair
15. recall

Page 13
Nouns only: resources
Verbs only: remember, rename
Adjectives only: recent, remarkable
Both nouns and verbs: result, regards, repair, recall, rewrite
Both nouns and adjectives: relief
Both verbs and adjectives: reduced, required
All three: research

Page 14
1. prejudice
2. preschool
3. presents
4. preferred
5. prevent
6. preceding
7. prepaid
8. presence
9. pretend
10. prepared
11. preoccupied
12. precise
13. precaution
14. premature
15. predict

Page 15
words w/2 syllables:
 prepared, prevent, preferred, precise, presence, presents, pretend, predict, prepaid, preschool
words w/3 syllables:
 precaution, preceding, prejudice, premature
words w/4 syllables:
 preoccupied

Page 16
1. OK
2. connected
3. OK
4. concerned
5. controlling
6. OK
7. conflict
8. OK
9. conversation
10. concert
11. OK
12. OK

Answer Key (cont.)

13. container
14. OK
15. construction

Page 17
1. concerned
2. controlling
3. convinced
4. consider
5. conditions
6. concert
7. connected
8. container
9. contact
10. continue
11. conversation
12. conserve
13. conflict
14. construction
15. contribute

Page 18
1. optimistic
2. mechanic
3. characteristics
4. realistic
5. assistant
6. historic
7. electronic
8. picnic
9. traffic
10. exists
11. distant
12. specific
13. automatic
14. insisted
15. scientist

Page 19

Page 20
1. foolish
2. English
3. distinguish
4. establish
5. publish
6. furnish
7. astonished
8. punish
9. selfish
10. relish
11. vanish
12. accomplish
13. Spanish
14. polish
15. diminish

Page 21
Answers will vary.

Page 22
1. photocopier *or* pier
2. hazard
3. afterwards
4. toward
5. soldier
6. orchard
7. awkward
8. standard
9. barrier
10. cupboard
11. glacier
12. cashier
13. forward
14. frontier
15. pier *or* photocopier

Page 23
1. antonym
2. antonym
3. antonym
4. synonym
5. antonym
6. antonym
7. synonym
8. synonym
9. synonym
10. antonym
11. antonym
12. synonym
13. antonym
14. synonym
15. synonym

Page 24
1. OK
2. positive
3. OK
4. OK
5. adjective
6. OK
7. attractive
8. negative
9. OK
10. executive
11. OK
12. sensitive
13. OK
14. OK
15. native

Page 25
1. motive
2. representatives
3. executive
4. relatives
5. competitive
6. negative
7. attractive
8. detective
9. effective
10. sensitive
11. adjective
12. active
13. talkative
14. positive
15. native

Riddle: Skunks. They'll give anyone a (s)cent.

Page 26
1. extravagant
2. important
3. relevant
4. elegant
5. hydrant
6. immigrant
7. servant
8. fragrant
9. significant
10. brilliant
11. infant
12. constant
13. restaurant
14. instant
15. pleasant

Page 27
1. antonym
2. antonym
3. antonym
4. antonym
5. synonym
6. synonym
7. antonym
8. antonym
9. synonym
10. synonym
11. antonym
12. synonym
13. synonym
14. antonym
15. antonym

Page 28
1. glance; 9; advance
2. chance; 6; ambulance
3. advance; 1; appearance
4. distance; 7; appliance
5. instance; 12; balance
6. balance; 5; chance
7. ambulance; 2; distance
8. appearance; 3; entrance
9. importance; 11; glance
10. performance; 13; guidance
11. resistance; 14; importance
12. entrance; 8; instance
13. tolerance; 15; performance
14. appliance; 4; resistance
15. guidance; 10; tolerance

Page 29
Answers will vary based on dictionary used.

Page 30
1. moisture
2. captured
3. miniature
4. temperature
5. signature
6. nature
7. future
8. furniture
9. literature
10. adventure
11. structure
12. creatures
13. mixture
14. features
15. agriculture

Answer Key (cont.)

Page 31

on "2" cymbal:
- nature
- future
- mixture
- captured
- features
- creatures
- structure
- moisture

on "3" cymbal:
- signature
- furniture
- adventure

on "4" cymbal:
- temperature
- miniature
- agriculture
- literature

Page 32
1. quantity
2. authority
3. opportunity
4. capacity
5. community
6. responsibility
7. ability
8. gravity
9. university
10. electricity
11. majority
12. similarity
13. curiosity
14. personality
15. quality

Page 33
1. gravity
2. quality
3. opportunity
4. university
5. curiosity
6. capacity
7. quantity
8. authority
9. personality
10. community
11. similarity
12. responsibility
13. electricity
14. ability
15. majority

Riddle: Boy, have I got problems!

Page 34
1. burglar
2. similar
3. solar
4. popular
5. molar
6. caterpillar
7. particular
8. polar
9. dollars
10. irregular
11. cellar
12. spectacular
13. regular
14. collar
15. cellular

Page 35
Answers will vary based on dictionary used.

Page 36
1. hopeful
2. successful
3. doubtful
4. powerful
5. thankful
6. beautiful
7. cheerful
8. painful
9. plentiful
10. useful
11. graceful
12. wonderfu
13. harmful
14. peaceful
15. awful

Page 37

second column:
1. full of awe
2. full of beauty
3. full of use
4. full of wonder
5. full of power
6. full of success
7. full of cheer
8. full of peace
9. full of doubt
10. full of pain
11. full of harm
12. full of thanks
13. full of hope
14. full of plenty
15. full of grace
16. When you add to "ful" to plenty and beauty, you change the "y" to an "i."

Page 38
1. OK
2. convenient
3. OK
4. continent
5. OK
6. different
7. current
8. OK
9. OK
10. accident
11. OK
12. OK
13. silent
14. OK
15. recent

Page 39
Answers will vary.

Page 40
1. sentence; 15; absence
2. difference; 5; audience
3. influence; 8; conference
4. audience; 2; convenience
5. reference; 13; different
6. evidence; 6; evidence
7. absence; 1; experience
8. experience; 7; influence
9. conference; 3; intelligence
10. occurrence; 10; occurrence
11. science; 14; patience
12. patience; 11; preference
13. preference; 12; reference
14. intelligence; 9; science
15. convenience; 4; sentence

Page 41

(Crossword: absence, science, reference, intelligence, patience, occurrence, convenience, existence, difference, preference, audience, influence)

Page 42
1. librarian
2. various
3. mysterious
4. cafeteria
5. historian
6. luxurious
7. obvious
8. previous
9. bacteria
10. hilarious
11. curious
12. vegetarian
13. furious
14. serious
15. encyclopedia

Page 43

nouns: bacteria, cafeteria, encyclopedia, librarian, vegetarian, historian

adjectives: various, curious, serious, obvious, furious, hilarious, luxurious, mysterious, previous

Page 44
1. d
2. c
3. e
4. a
5. c
6. b
7. a
8. c
9. b
10. d
11. b
12. e
13. c
14. a
15. d
16. b
17. e
18. c
19. a
20. d

Page 45
1. e
2. a
3. d
4. e
5. c
6. d
7. b
8. c
9. a
10. b
11. c
12. a
13. e
14. e
15. d
16. b
17. c
18. d
19. b
20. a